# THE KNEES KNOCK AGAIN

For Hinda —
Wishing you joy
and a giggle!

Carolyn Lesser
. 91

by Carolyn Lesser
illustrated by Larry Shles

FOR LARRY,
ENCOURAGING FRIEND
EXCEPTIONAL COLLABORATOR.
THANK YOU.
C.L.

Many of our ideas come from children and adults we meet as we travel the country, encouraging educators and students to read, write, and enjoy their own creativity. We thank all those who have so generously shared their ideas and encouraged us to do another book.

# THE KNEES
# KNOCK AGAIN

by Carolyn Lesser
illustrated by Larry Shles

Oakwood Press
St. Louis, MO.

## MY WORD-WORLD

Come into my word-world of fancy.
Let my words make you shiver, dance, and sing.
Take a look inside you. Find a friend, perhaps two.
Listen! The knees knock again!

Come open the door of your wonderful mind.
Hear music, see pictures words bring.
Leap up flying free, to a star, 'cross the sea.
Listen! The knees knock again!

## SUMMER TUNE

Now June
Pool boon
Grill fume
Hot noon
Hose flume
Sand dune
Big moon
Night loon
Over soon.

## SUMMER DAY

Come slide and slop and slap and slip
In ploppin', droppin', splattin' drips!

Running, leaping, Whoops! I fell!
Jumping, giggling, laughing, Yell!

The sprinkler's on! Get wet and wild!
It's screamin'-steamin' summer, child!

## SOLO

The sandpipers prance primly
Along the water's edge
Until golden sunrise-waves,
Freckled with glittering crystal,
Race in to tickle their toes.
Startled, they run from giggles
To the safety of dunes and beach grass.
All except one.

At dusk pink sunset-waves hiss
Back into the endless sea
As the tide still reaches
For that one pair of twiggy legs
Dancing,
A hairbreadth out of reach,
On the glistening-chilling beach.
In her solitary wake
She leaves tiny footprints
And grace.

## A NIGHT ON THE TOWN

"Hi cutie!" said the bat swooping down.
"How about a night out on the town?
 I could float you near Mars,
 We'd see millions of stars.
 Come with me. I'm a bat of renown!"

"Dear bat," said the mouse with concern,
"My cousin you dated, I learned.
 To date a brown bat
 Is much worse than a cat.
 My small cousin has never returned!"

"Sweet mouse," said the bat with a hoot,
"I'm wise, handsome, strong and astute.
 I have elegant squeeks.
 You have cute, tiny cheeks.
 I'm in love!
 I'll romance you for weeks!"

Now, the bat was a wondrous sight,
His eyes gleaming red in the night.
Oh, to fly! thought the mouse,
Over fields, stream, and house,
Is worth chancing a terrible bite.

She climbed on his back with a hop.
Up he flew over hills to the top
Of the mountain so high,
In the silver-starred sky.
"I love flying!" she crooned.
"Never stop!"

Oh his heart, it was in the right place.
But it couldn't compete with his face.
As he flew  his teeth ached
For a mouse souffle baked
Served with sauce, on a table with lace.

"Hold onto my neck! Hang on tight!"
"I will!" cried Miss Mouse, with delight.
He did loops, spins, and flips
She slid nearer his lips.
I'm a bat, not a Prince!
Drool! Chomp! Bite!!!

As he bit,
Great fear caused her to slip
Off his back, on a fast earthbound trip.
But dear lucky Miss Mouse
Tumbled in a bird's house
Snug and warm, and she did a cute flip!

Miss Mouse from a nest now looks down
And remembers
Her night on the town.
The bat was entrancing!
The flight felt like dancing!
No regrets, she smiles, fluffing her gown.

# FIVE SHAGGY LLAMAS

There was a fine chef from Peru,
Who cooked for five llamas ... it's true!
He whipped up slime cake, candied liver, fried snake,
For the shaggy five loved slurping goo.

## I HAB A CODE

I hab a code id by dose
Ad I cad pway today.
Baby I cad pway tobow-woe.

I wand to wud ad jumb ad skib
Bud here I ab stuck id bed,
Stufd wid bedicine,
YUK!

I hab a code id by dose
Ad I cad pway today,
Bud ....
I ab GOIG to pway tobow-woe!

## FIRST GRADE

I have a weird thing in my mouth
Hanging by a string.
Since I got it, it has made first grade
Real interesting.

When everyone is working hard
The room becomes too quiet.
Then my tooth and I get busy
And create a silent riot!

My tongue can push and pull my tooth
Almost .... nearly .... out.
My fingers whirl it, twirl it, swirl it
All around-about.

I rock it, roll it, in and out,
Then stick it back in place.
I love my floppy, flippy tooth.
It's OUT?
I love my face!

## SNAZZY-JAZZY FLUFF

Ruby, Pearl, and Sapphire were
Gleaming in the night,
Rocking on the bandstand,
Shining in the light,

Scattin', chattin', waa-be-do,
Doo-wop-be-bop-shoo-be-doo,
Singin', playin' tunes like mad,
Be-bop-doo-wop, feelin' glad!

So romp it, stomp it,
Rock it, jam!
What snazzy-jazzy fluff, you am!

# MISS GERTRUDE NEAT and TEN-EIGHTEEN

There it was, old 1018.
There she stood mad and mean.
The woman we called the eighth grade pain,
(The aide we'd love to send to Spain)
Took us out there in the hall,
Lined us up facing the wall.
"Get busy! No talking! Stop your play!
Vacation starts in just one day.
I want these lockers clean!" yelled
Miss Gertrude Neat.

We popped our locks and out things flew,
Rotted bananas, cooking class stew,
Chewed gum stuck to book reports,
Stiff and crusty socks and shorts,
Snickers flattened between shoes and tapes,
Frisbees, yo-yo's, my paper on apes,
Black and furry science class beans
Wound 'round ear muffs, purple and green.
"I've never seen such a sloppy class!" screamed
Miss Gert Neat.

We threw our stuff into a heap.
Our junk piled up six feet deep
With sleeping bags and canteens filled
With stuff so thick it couldn't spill,
Copies of novels we didn't read,
There's Jennifer's goldfish I didn't feed,
Wads of paper, crumpled tests,
Movie stars we liked the best,
Hairspray, softball gloves and bats,
Ugly winter gloves and hats.

At last we did it. Each locker was clean
Thanks to Miss Neat, nasty and mean.
Now the hall was a mess, but the hall was quiet.
Gert's voice was gone. It was quiet, quiet, quiet.

Then I stared at the pile and began to grin
For Gert's feet stuck out, bony and thin.
We whooped and cheered, "She's gone at last,
That obnoxious voice is mashed.
Lucky eighth grade! Good going lockers!
You GOT her with our trash!"

## DRAGONFLY

Dragonfly alights softly
on purple fluff, hidden swords.
Thistlestop courage.

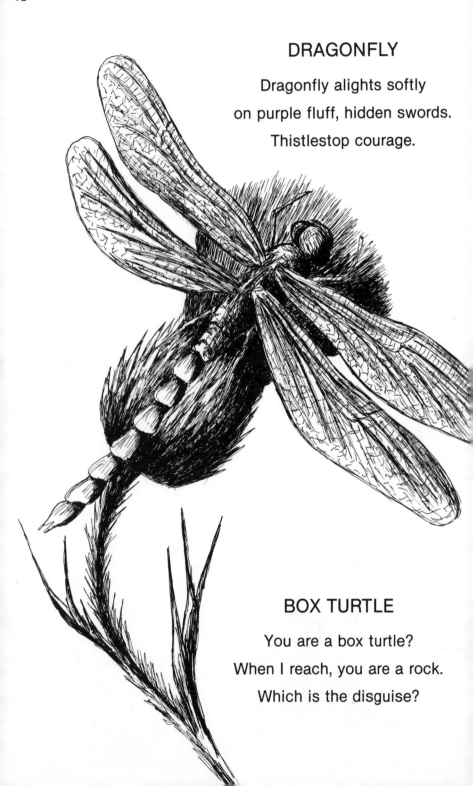

## BOX TURTLE

You are a box turtle?
When I reach, you are a rock.
Which is the disguise?

## FOREST VISIT

Some hot sunny day
Walk into woods of dappled light.

Take eyes that see tiny things,
Ears tuned to quiet.

Rest on this earth, silent in silence,
Your body still as a fallen tree.

Look!
A spider on stilts
Tiptoeing across dry leaves.

Listen!
Whispery footsteps
And your heartbeat.

## CUB COURAGE

I'm looking mom, watching like you.
I love the things I see,
Grasses blowing, clouds, blue sky.
I want to explore. Can we?

What do you see? Your eyes look wary.
Should I hide? Is danger near?
Your lovely rumble is turning to growl,
But I still want to play. I've no fear.

Yet to stay alive I must do what you do.
I must watch and learn and try
To hide and hunt,
To prowl and fight.
But the sky, how I love the sky!

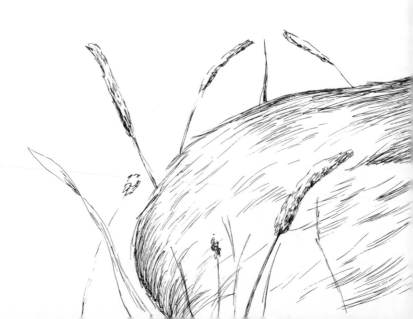

## MARY MARGARET'S PIANO PRACTICE

I play "The Spinning Wheel" over and over
And over and over again.
And she says at each lesson,
"It is improving.
One more week,
It will be perfect then."

But picky Miss Woodland does not understand.
I bet she was never a kid.
I don't want it perfect,
I just want it different,
Like the next song, "Sunny Madrid".

She says I have talent, might play in a concert
If I practiced each day, real long.
But who'd buy a ticket?
Who'd come to a concert
When all they would hear is one song?

# BUGS

Beetles,
Bees,
Wasps and flies,

Stingers,
Feelers,
Wings and eyes,

Flying, jumping,
Crawling slow,

When I see you,
I go — GO ——GO!

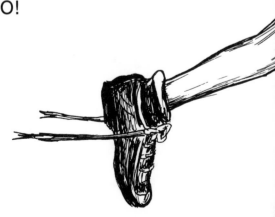

# DOOLEY

A leaper,
A licker,
A lapper,
My dog.

A roller,
A runner,
A racer,
My dog.

A shaker,
A shedder,
A slurper,
My dog.

I love him,
The fuzz him,
Great Dooley
My dog.

## MUFFIN'S WISHES

'Round and 'round, faster and faster,
Spinning, careening free
The wheel turns, then slows and stops
With wonderful treasures for me.

What will I choose, the glassy-eyed dog,
The barbecue grill or the trips
To Hawaii, Peru or Timbuktu
Or the sparkling diamond clip?

So here I sprawl, my hopes flying high,
While my ears droop limp and low.
I dream of prizes on "The Wheel of Fortune".
Oh how I love that show!

# RINGO FLAMINGO

Ringo Flamingo dug jazz-jazzy lingo,
Dug it and rapped it all day.
"Like man, what a gas! This gig is like rockin'!
The beat out of sight! Man, let's play!"

So hushin' and brushin' trompin' the pedal,
Rappin' and flippin' the sticks,
Ringo Flamingo hit bongos, beat snare drums,
Gave cymbals some jazz-jazzy licks.

"Like man, this is rockin'!" said Ringo Flamingo,
Boppin' and rappin' his beat.
So the jazz-jazzy Ringo, that Ringo Flamingo,
Said, "Go man, I dig it, it's sweet!"

## HUMPERDINK'S LAMENT

I'm last in line and getting laster.
My heart is beating fast, then faster.
I'm supposed to dive into the sea.
Be what a penguin's supposed to be.
But even when I think I'll jump
My feet don't move.
I'm like a stump.

## HUMPERDINK'S DISCOVERY

I'm still watching, but now I've got fins
Just in case I decide I do want to swim.
I'll go to the absolute top of the hill
For I think very clearly in that kind of chill.

Oh-oh, this hill seems icy and slick.
Climbing in fins to the top is a trick.
Whoa .... I'm starting to slip and slide downhill fast!
Hey! It's fun!
Two .... Three .... Dive!

## HUMPERDINK'S VICTORY

Now I am bobbing up like the rest.
Some even say I am one of the best.
I swim and slide, I dive soaring high.
It's hard to believe I did not want to try.

Then a lucky accident slid me into the sea.
Scary at first, but lucky for me,
For I found I can float.
I can swim. I can dive.
I'm a penguin, a penguin,
Brave and alive!

# DAYDREAMS

Sometimes I feel so quiet inside
I sit and stare and dream
Of growing up or staying small
And all the in-between.

I'd be a knight, slash silver swords
At dragons shimmering green,
All fire and flash, bash and crash,
In lands I've never seen.

Perhaps I'd be the captain
Of the finest fleet in space,
All shining stars, Neptune, Mars,
My sleek-slick way to race.

I'd be a dad with seven kids
Playing in the park,
All strength and hugs, catch lightning bugs,
Tell stories in the dark.

Sometimes I feel so quiet inside,
I sit and stare and dream
Of growing up or staying small
And all the in-between.

# DAYDREAMS

Sometimes I feel so quiet inside,
I sit and stare and dream
Of growing up or staying small
And all the in-between.

I'm princess of Rose Castle
With cats and horses inside.
All sparkly crowns and billowy gowns,
Hair flying free, I'd ride.

Perhaps I'd be the captain
Of the finest fleet in space,
All shining stars, Neptune, Mars,
My sleek-slick way to race.

I'd be a mom, rock babies warm,
Tuck my children in at night,
All soft and strong, sing dancy songs,
Explore, read, draw, and write.

Sometimes I feel so quiet inside,
I sit and stare and dream
Of growing up or staying small
And all the in-between.

## MUFFIN'S BUNCH

Ears like propellers in a breeze
Point north and south, nice as you please.
East and west and all around,
Baby lops flopped on the ground.

Ears like clockhands tick and tock
To ten-fifteen and three o'clock,
Nine-o-six and two-o-three.
I want every baby lop I see.

# "THE CREEP", THE FROGS, and ME

Frogs make me shiver.
I'm not kidding, they do.
They're slippery and slimy,
Dripping mud too.

But, my brother, "The Creep",
Says, "Wow! This is fun!"
He catches a bunch,
Looks for me, starts to run.

He chases me,
Dangles big frogs in my face.
I scream and I run
In that wild, scary race,
For the frogs hanging near,
With the big bulgy eyes,
Smell just like a swamp
From their diet of flies.

I'll take a big spider,
A boa, a bat,
A tiger, a sister,
A lizard, a rat.
I'll climb up a cliff or crawl in a cave.
I'll dive off the highboard.
I'm gutsy and brave!

But, you take my brother.
Take the frogs large and small.
I won't miss that wild scary chase.
Not at all!

WAIT ... !
Take the vile frogs, but please,
Leave my brother.
He's "The Creep"
And my best friend.
I don't want another.

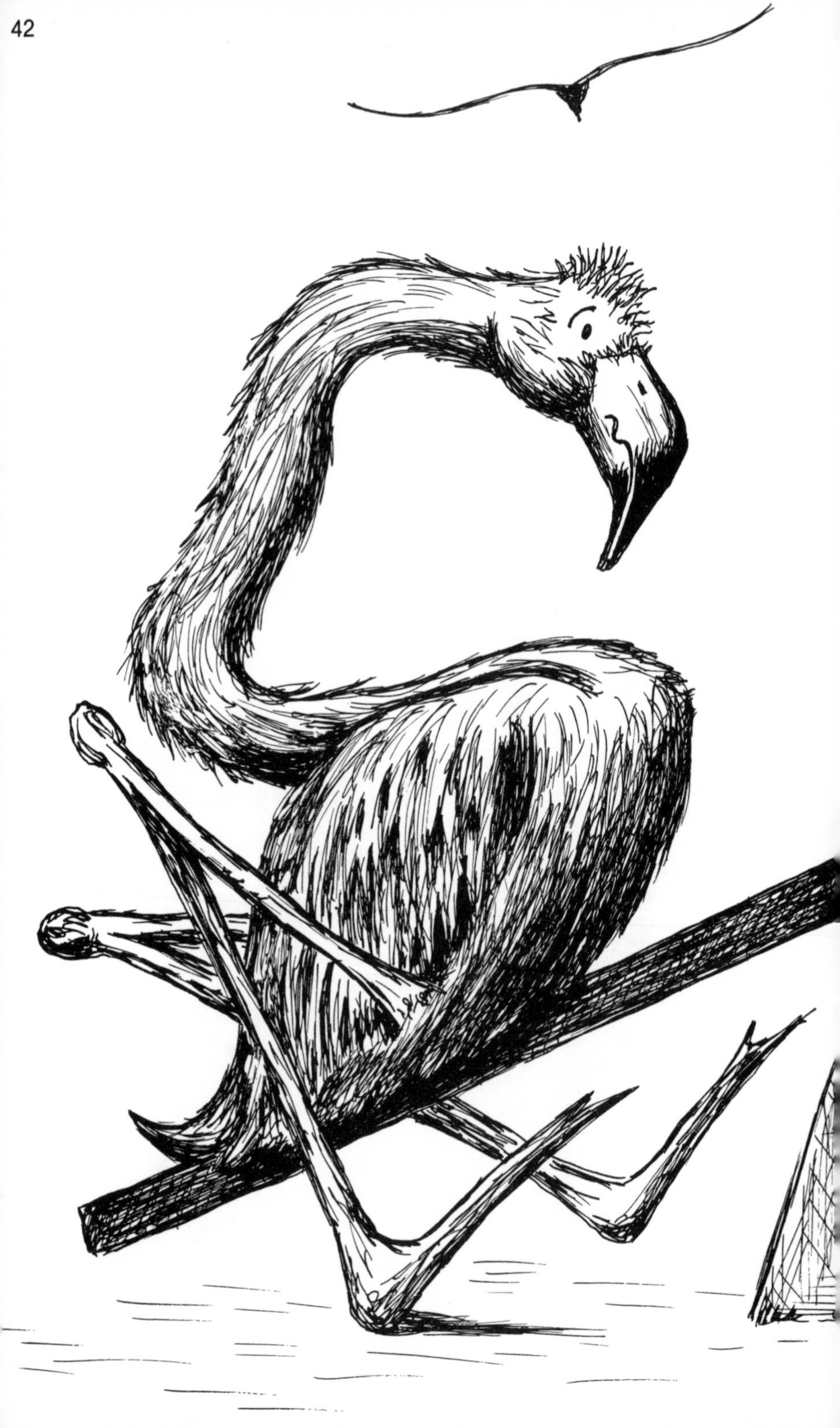

## UP TO THE SKY AND DOWN

See-saw, see-saw,
Up and down all day.
Friends in pairs taking dares,
Bounce up and down to play.

But here I am ... I'm only down!
I need a friend right now
To come along and pop me up.
I'd settle for a cow.

Hi Victor! Verne! Vera! Vince!
Hey! I'm leaving the ground!
Vinnie, come on! I love this trip,
Up to the sky and down!

## I LOVE MY THESAURUS

I love my thesaurus, or do I mean like,
Or fancy, adore, or regard?
With list after list
Of such interesting words
My decisions are often quite hard.

I used to write, 'He walked into the room'.
"Dull!" said my teacher, Miss Campbell,
"Try this book,
You'll see there are choices galore!"
I read, march, parade, hike, and ramble.

"So what do you mean?
What do you want to say?" she asked,
Her smile wide and charming.
I just wanted the man to get in the room,
Then I thought ... Here is power alarming!

With so many words he does not have to walk.
I can make him stroll, trudge, or drop.
I turned the pages.
Read, bum, wampum, rages.
It was hopeless. I just couldn't stop!

Each page held a treasure,
Like sloppy or slob,
Frump, dolt, or slovenly swine,
Flim-flam, bunk, hooey,
Humbug and phooey.
What jewels! Gems soon to be mine!

As days went by I read
Google, gape, ghoulish.
Wrote, gawking, grope,
Warpaint, and nook.
Tried toll, peal, ring-jingle,
Quaver, quake, tingle,
Brain bewitched by the miraculous book.

For words, lovely words,
Can paint fanciful pictures
With strokes raring-daring, brave-bold.
Thesaurus! Thesaurus!
My friend and companion,
What astonishing stories we've told!

# MOUSE-CATCHERS, HEART-SNATCHERS

Kittens for sale! Kittens for sale!
Soft furry pink-nosed kittens for sale!
Just five dollars each.
What a deal! What a steal!
Mouse-catching-heart-snatching kittens
For sale!

Kittens for sale! Kittens for sale!
Lap-sitting-snuggle-purring kittens
For sale! Just two dollars each.
What a deal! What a steal!
Mouse-catching-heart-snatching kittens
For sale!

Kittens for sale! Kittens for sale!
Strong-muscled-fierce-hunting kittens
For sale!
Only cost you a dollar. A quarter?
A dime? What a steal! What a deal!
Mouse-catching-heart-snatching kittens
For sale!

I guess no one needs any kittens today
'Cause I've walked and talked and told and ...
... WOW!
This means all the soft-furry-pink-nosed,
Lap-sitting-cuddle-purring,
Strong-muscled-fierce-hunting,
Mouse-catching-heart-snatching kittens
Are mine!

What a deal! What a steal!
Lucky day! Lucky me!
And just think,
I got all these great kittens
Free!

# MANGLED, TANGLED, ANGLES

I love the jungle gym at school.
I play with Pete, my friend.
Up and down, in and out,
But who knows where I end?

I loop and dip, swoop and slip.
Is that my neck or my feet?
My beak is where? My wing, over there?
"Pearl! Come on up!" calls Pete.

"Pete!" said Pearl, "I cannot move!
I'm mangled, tangled, angles."
Said Pete to Pearl, "You're my best girl.
I'll come down there and dangle!"

LARGE

Large cat.

Large rat ...

# Larger cat!

## SEVEN TINY SNAILS

Seven tiny snails creeping
On a twig ...

The first one said,
"I wish I was big."

The second one said,
"I wish I could sing."

The third one said,
"I want a ruby ring."

The fourth one said,
"I'd love to leap and dive!"

The fifth one said,
"How great to be alive!"

The sixth one said,
"I crave a chocolate cake."

The seventh one said,
"Look out! Here comes a sna___!!!

# FLYING FREE

To fly on a flowered carpet
Riding the breeze wild and free,
To go anywhere I wanted
Oh, that'd be the life for me!

I'd want to fly over the ocean,
Over dolphins and whales and squid
Above jungles with tigers and parrots,
Zoom 'round castle spires in Madrid.

I'd swoop over sparkling icebergs,
Over rivers that rush to the sea,
Past deserts and dunes, ruins and tombs
Then at last to the Isle To-Be-Me.

There I'd rest and play until one day
The wind would call to me.
Then my carpet and I would rise in the sky
Flying free! Oh yes, flying free!

# THE JOURNEY

I love that you've joined in my song
As we wandered roads winding and long.
We began as unknown,
But look how we've grown to be friends
As we travelled along.

It's lovely, you're here now with me.
Take my hand, we're together yet free.
Words made us one, but we've only begun.
Dream your dreams. Dance your dance.
Dare to be.